Album FOR THE Young

64 PIANO CLASSICS WRITTEN BY THE MASTERS

Published by:
CHESTER MUSIC LIMITED,
14-15 Berners Street, London, W1T 3LJ, UK.

Exclusive Distributors:
MUSIC SALES LIMITED
Distribution Centre, Newmarket Road,
Bury St Edmunds, Suffolk, IP33 3YB, UK.
MUSIC SALES CORPORATION
180 Madison Avenue, 24th Floor,
New York, NY 10016, USA.
MUSIC SALES PTY LIMITED
Units 3-4, 17 Willfox Street, Condell Park,
NSW 2200, Australia.

Order No. CH82632
ISBN 978-1-78305-379-7
This book © Copyright 2014 by Chester Music.

Compiled and edited by Sam Lung.
Music processed by Camden Music Services,
Elius Gravure Musicale and Paul Ewers Music Design.
Cover designed by Adela Casacuberta.
Printed in the EU.

Your Guarantee of Quality:

As publishers, we strive to produce every book
to the highest commercial standards.

The music has been freshly engraved and the book has been carefully designed to
minimise awkward page turns and to make playing from it a real pleasure.

Particular care has been given to specifying acid-free, neutral-sized paper
made from pulps which have not been elemental chlorine bleached.
This pulp is from farmed sustainable forests and was produced
with special regard for the environment.

Throughout, the printing and binding have been planned to ensure a sturdy,
attractive publication which should give years of enjoyment.

If your copy fails to meet our high standards, please inform us
and we will gladly replace it.

www.musicsales.com

CHESTER MUSIC
part of The Music Sales Group

London / New York / Paris / Sydney / Copenhagen / Berlin / Madrid / Hong Kong / Tokyo

Two-part Invention No.4 in D Minor

Johann Sebastian Bach

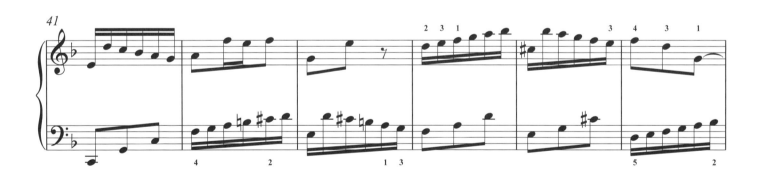

Two-part Invention No.8 in F Major

JOHANN SEBASTIAN BACH

Sonatina in G Major

1st movement

Ludwig van Beethoven

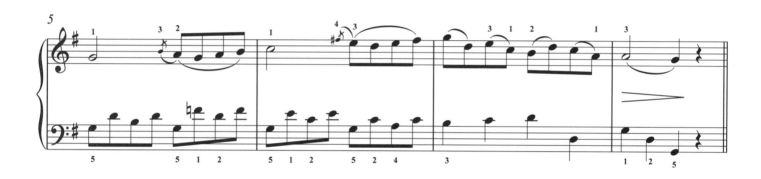

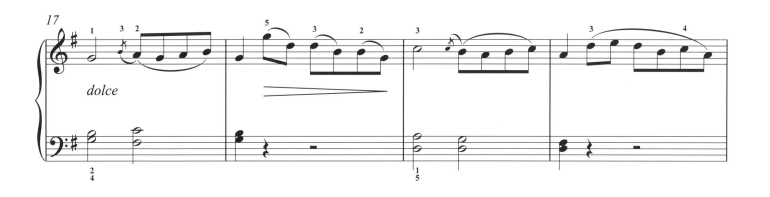

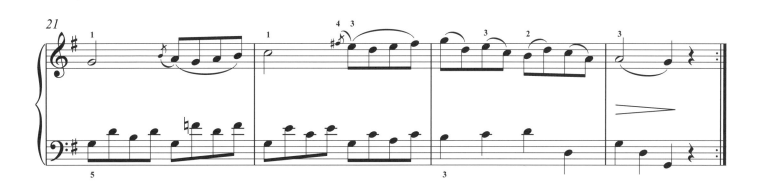

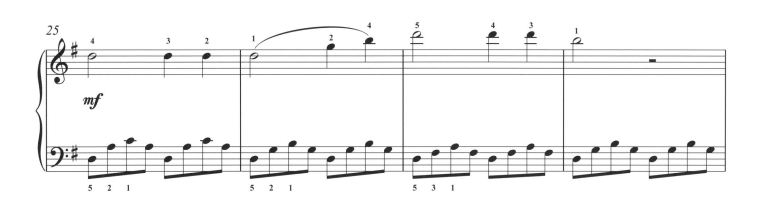

Two Turtle Doves

from Partridge Pie

RICHARD RODNEY BENNETT

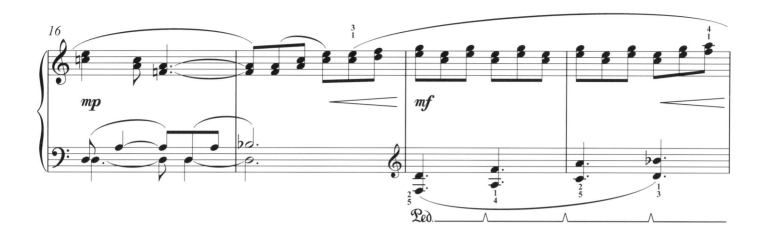

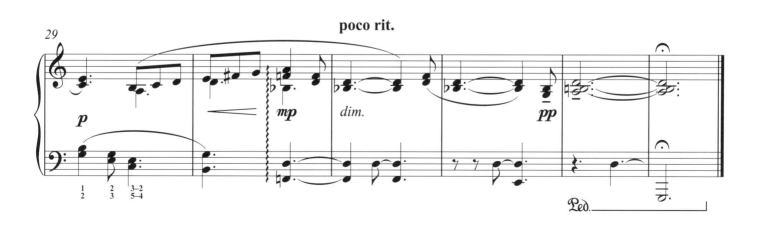

Eight Maids a-Milking

from Partridge Pie

Richard Rodney Bennett

Mr Pilkington's Toye

LENNOX BERKELEY

Wiegenlied (Cradle Song)

JOHANNES BRAHMS

langsamer

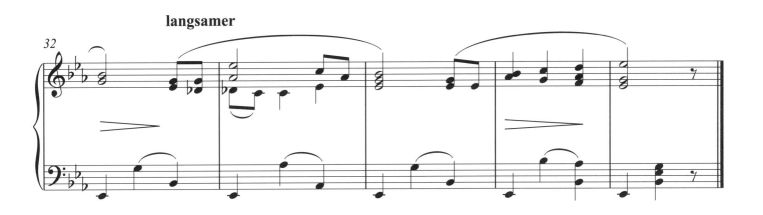

The Blue Pool

from On The Cool Side

Brian Chapple

Far From Home

from In The Pink

Brian Chapple

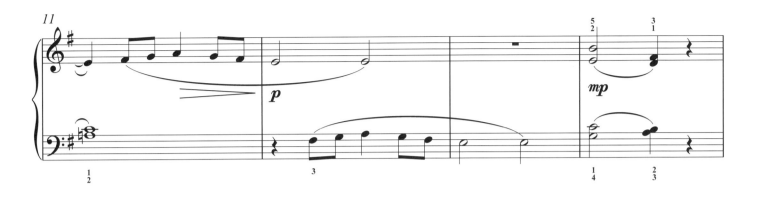

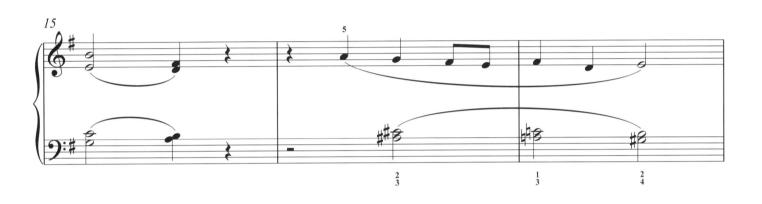

The Snow Melts

from Lazy Days

Brian Chapple

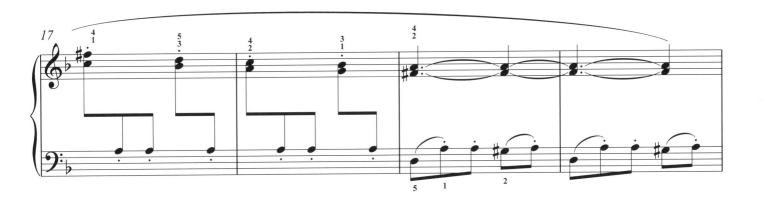

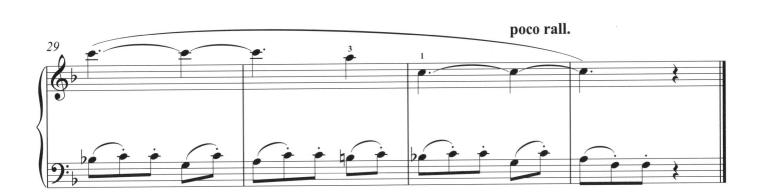

The Little Shepherd

from Children's Corner

CLAUDE DEBUSSY

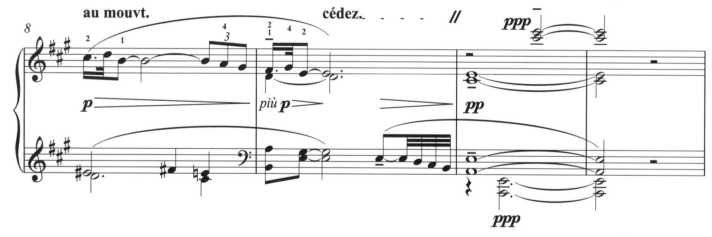

Melisandra

from Master Peter's Puppet Show

MANUEL DE FALLA

Molto lento e sostenuto ♪ = 100

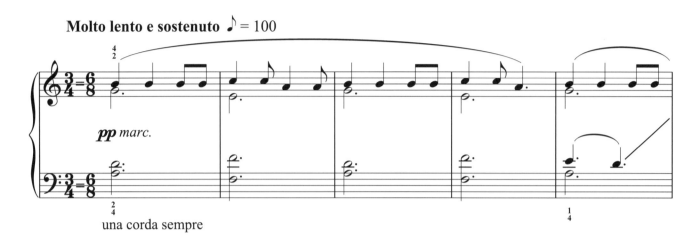

Molto lento e sostenuto ♪ = 100

pp marc.

una corda sempre

dolce marc. il canto

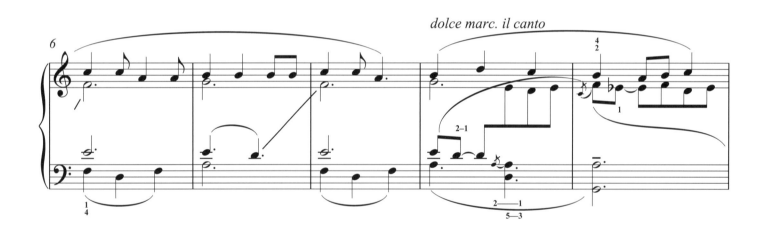

appena rit.   **tempo, ma sempre molto sostenuto**

misterioso

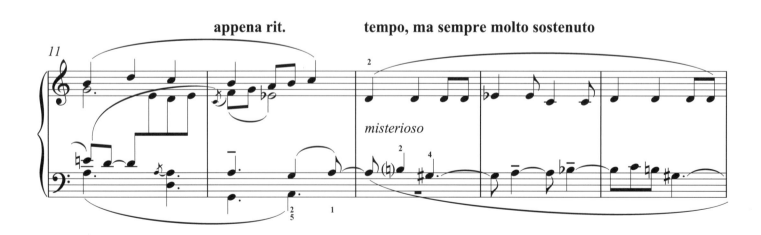

27

Berceuse

from Dolly Suite

GABRIEL FAURÉ

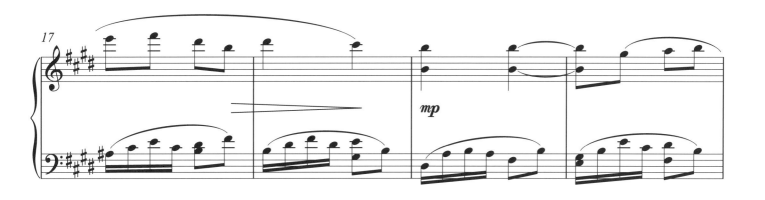

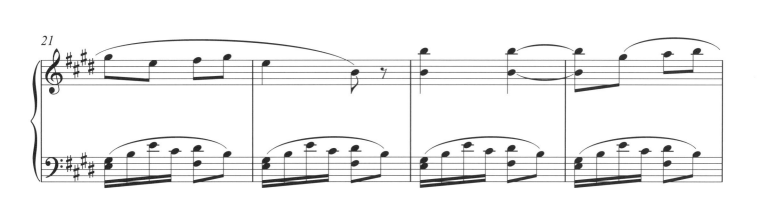

Lady Of Letters

from Lady Of Letters

George Fenton

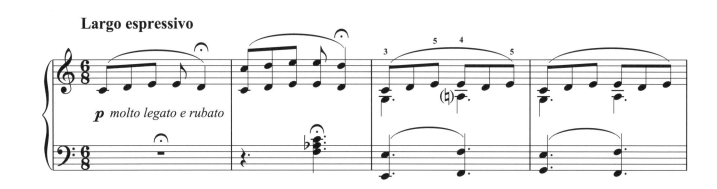

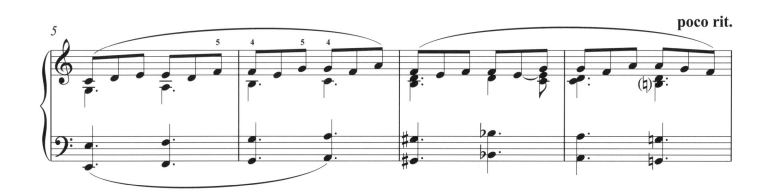

The Monocled Mutineer

from The Monocled Mutineer

GEORGE FENTON

Valse Triste

from The Cherry Orchard

George Fenton

Puppet's Complaint

(Doll's Lament)

César Franck

Wiegenlied (Cradle Song)

No.1 *from* Piano Transcriptions of Own Songs

Edvard Grieg

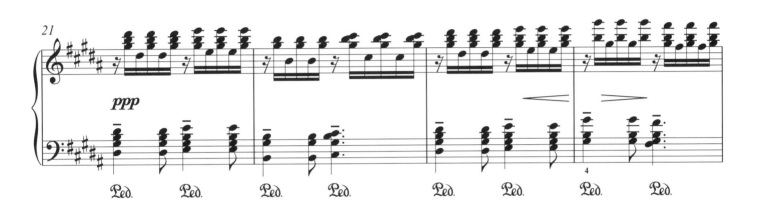

My Love She Was So Pure

No.4 *from* Piano Transcriptions of Own Songs

EDVARD GRIEG

Poco allegretto e semplice

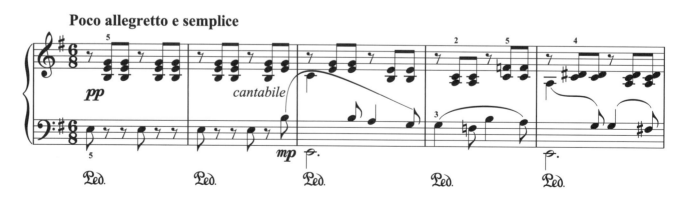

At Gellert's Grave

No.3 *from* 9 Children's Pieces

Edvard Grieg

Playful Dialogue

JOHANN NEPOMUK HUMMEL

Moderato

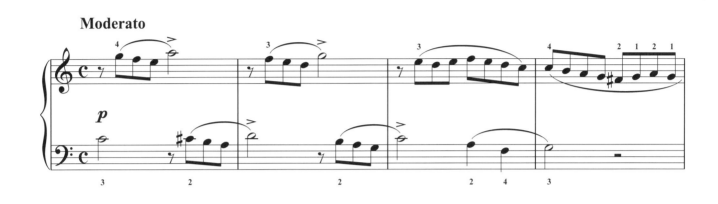

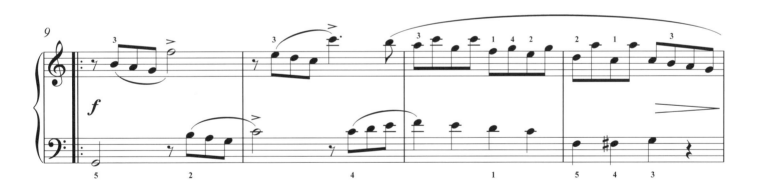

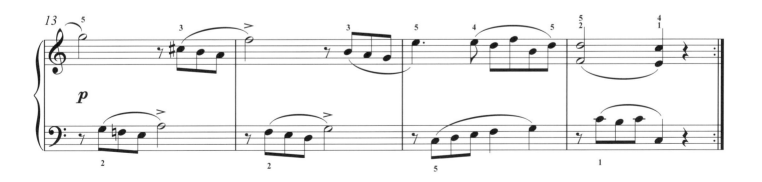

The Swan

from Pieces For Angela, Op.47

KENNETH LEIGHTON

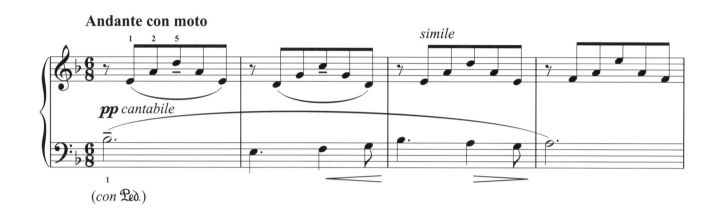

Étude en douze exercices, S.136

No.3

FRANZ LISZT

Allegro sempre legato ♩ = 80

Wiegenlied (Cradle Song)

S.198

FRANZ LISZT

Master Michael

No.7 *from* Folk Melodies

Witold Lutosławski

The Schoolmaster

No.12 *from* Folk Melodies

Witold Lutosławski

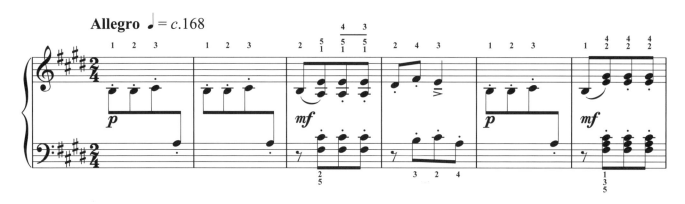

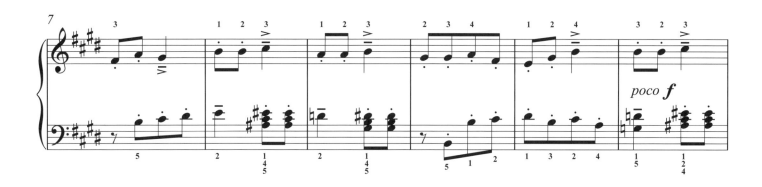

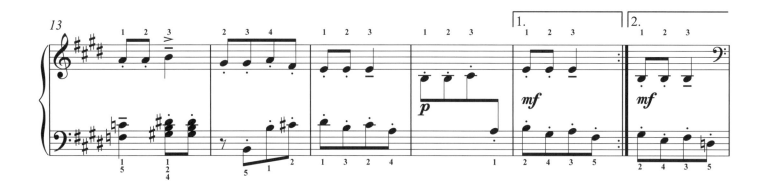

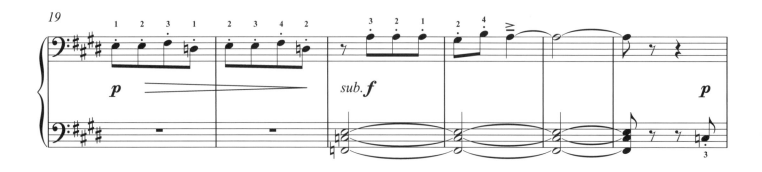

An Air

No.2 *from* Three Pieces For The Young

Witold Lutosławski

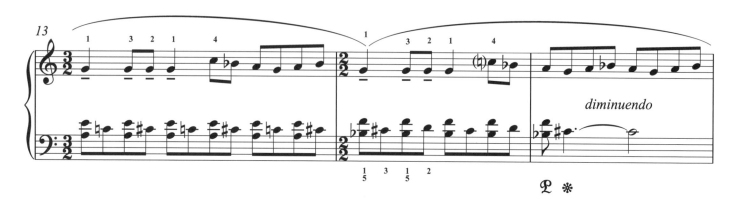

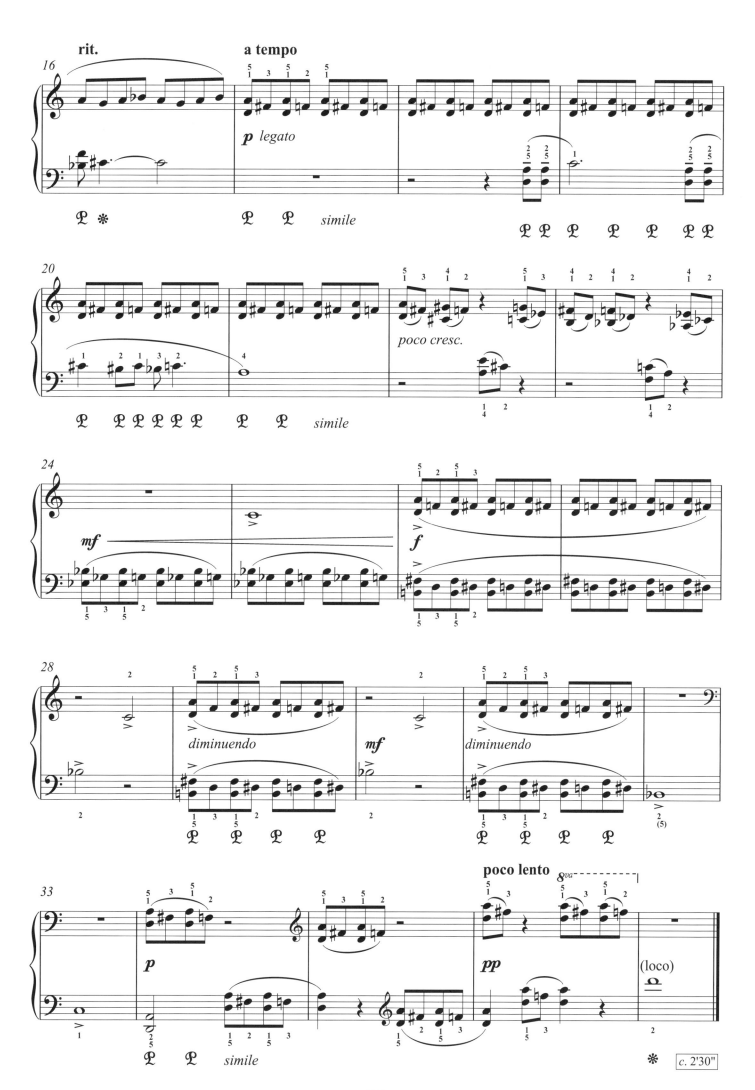

Bucolics

No.5

WITOLD LUTOSŁAWSKI

Aria

from Six Tunes For Lucy

COLIN MATTHEWS

Six Secret Songs

No.1

Peter Maxwell Davies

Andante

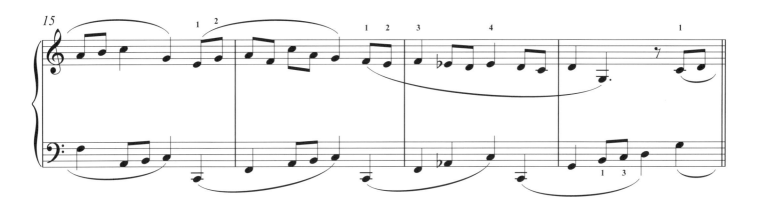

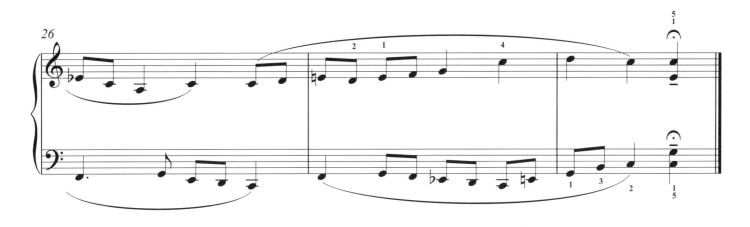

Six Pieces For Children, Op.72

(Six Christmas Pieces)

No.1

Felix Mendelssohn

Pessebres (Créches)

(Nativity Scene)

FEDERICO MOMPOU

Theme and Three Variations
on 'Ah, vous dirai-je, Maman'

K.265

Wolfgang Amadeus Mozart

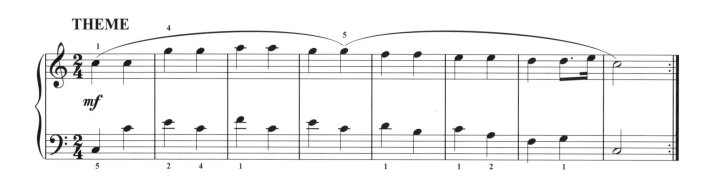

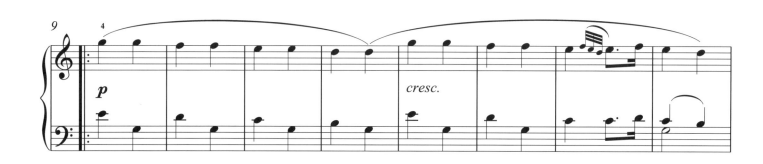

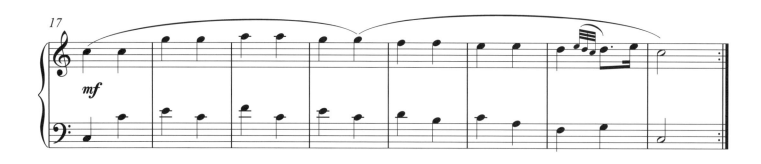

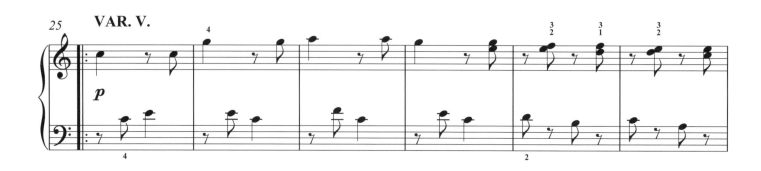

cresc. dim. *p*

VAR. VIII.
Minore

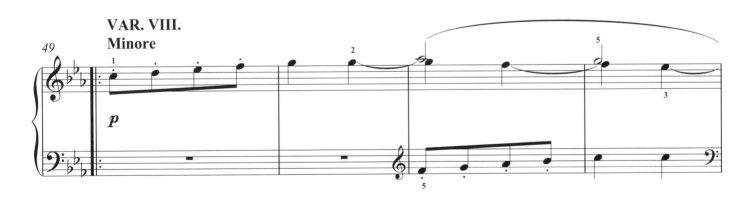

p

più f

71

Sonata in C Major, K.545

1st movement

WOLFGANG AMADEUS MOZART

Piano Music For Young And Old

No.1

CARL NIELSEN

The Story Of Babar, The Little Elephant

The Tea Shop

Francis Poulenc

Ensuite il les emmène chez le pâtissier manger de bons gâteaux.

Next he took them to a tea shop, where they had some delicious cakes.

sans ralentir

Pavane Of The Sleeping Beauty

from Mother Goose

MAURICE RAVEL

Pavane de la Belle au bois dormant

Lent ♩ = 58

The Young Prince And The Young Princess

from Scheherazade

Nikolai Rimsky-Korsakov

Prelude And Fugue No.4

from Five Miniature Preludes And Fugues

ALEC ROWLEY

FUGUE
Allegretto

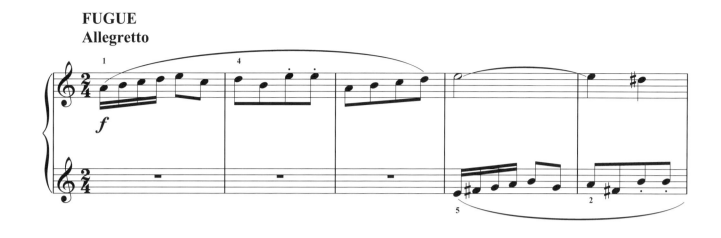

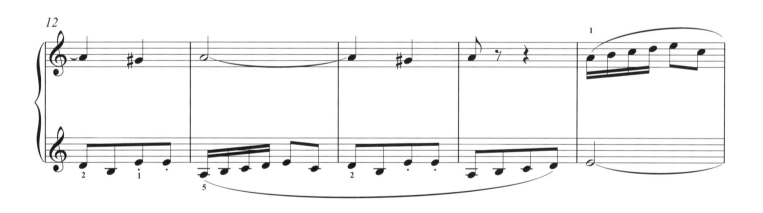

The Elephant

from The Carnival Of The Animals

CAMILLE SAINT-SAËNS

Ecossaise No.5

from Eight Ecossaises, D.977

Franz Schubert

Ecossaise No.8

from Eight Ecossaises, D.977

Franz Schubert

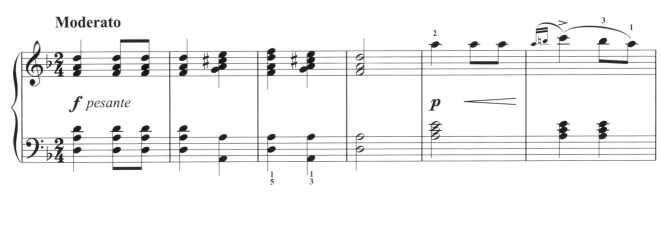

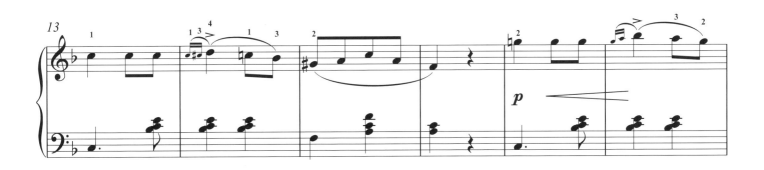

Melody

from Album For The Young

ROBERT SCHUMANN

Soldier's March

from Album For The Young

ROBERT SCHUMANN

Munter und straff

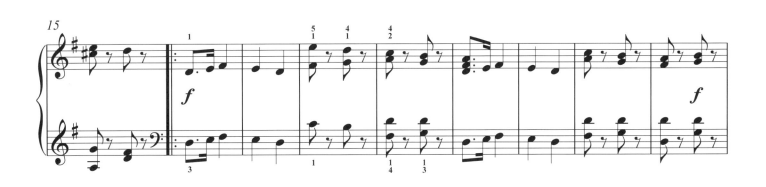

Humming Song

from Album For The Young

ROBERT SCHUMANN

Little Piece

from Album For The Young

ROBERT SCHUMANN

The Wild Horseman

from Album For The Young

Robert Schumann

Bewegt, doch nicht zu rasch

The Happy Farmer, Returning From Work

from Album For The Young

ROBERT SCHUMANN

Sicilienne

from Album For The Young

ROBERT SCHUMANN

Fine

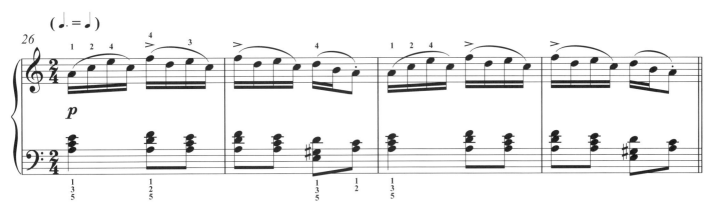

D.C. senza repetizione al Fine

101

Little Study

from Album For The Young

Robert Schumann

First Loss

from Album For The Young

Robert Schumann

Wintertime II

from Album For The Young

Robert Schumann

Nach und nach langsamer

Mignon

from Album For The Young

Robert Schumann

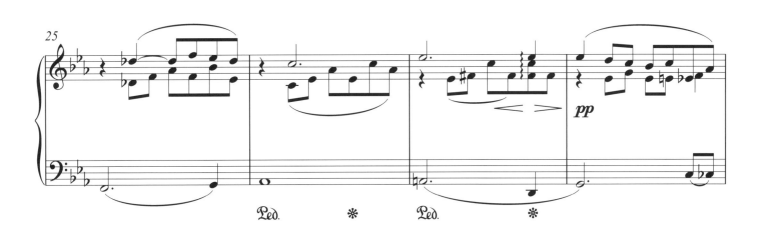

Of Foreign Lands And People

from Scenes From Childhood

ROBERT SCHUMANN

The Poet Speaks

from Scenes From Childhood

Robert Schumann

Frightening

from Scenes From Childhood

Robert Schumann

Waltz

from Three Easy Pieces

Igor Stravinsky

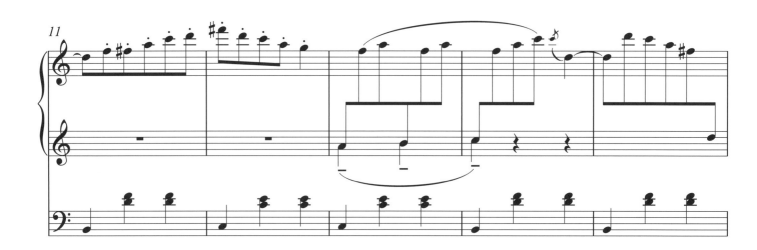

Les Cinq Doigts

No.1

IGOR STRAVINSKY

116

Dance Of The Sugar Plum Fairy

from The Nutcracker Suite

Pyotr Ilyich Tchaikovsky

119

Dance Of The Cygnets

from Swan Lake

Pyotr Ilyich Tchaikovsky

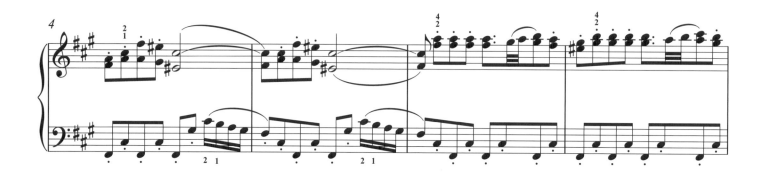

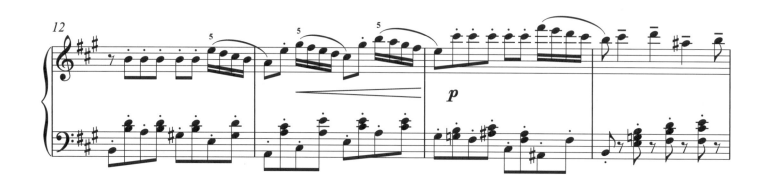

Maman

from Album For The Young

Pyotr Ilyich Tchaikovsky

poco ritard.

March Of The Wooden Soldiers

from Album For The Young

Pyotr Ilyich Tchaikovsky

125

The New Doll

from Album For The Young

Pyotr Ilyich Tchaikovsky

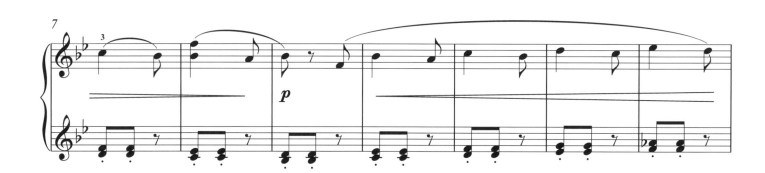

The Sick Doll

from Album For The Young

PYOTR ILYICH TCHAIKOVSKY

1 2 3 4 5 6 7 8 9